WITHDRAWN

Numbers and Counting

by Henry Pluckrose

Gareth Stevens Publishing
A WORLD ALMANAC EDUCATION GROUP COMPANY

Please visit our web site at: www.garethstevens.com
For a free color catalog describing Gareth Stevens' list of high-quality books
and multimedia programs, call 1-800-542-2595 (USA) or 1-800-461-9120 (Canada).
Gareth Stevens Publishing's Fax: (414) 332-3567.

Library of Congress Cataloging-in-Publication Data

Pluckrose, Henry Arthur.
   [How many are there?]
   Numbers and counting / by Henry Pluckrose. — North American ed.
     p. cm. — (Let's explore)
   Includes bibliographical references and index.
   ISBN 0-8368-2964-6 (lib. bdg.)
   1. Arithmetic—Juvenile literature. 2. Counting—Juvenile literature. [1. Arithmetic.
  2. Counting.] I. Title.
  QA115.P62 2001
  513.2'11—dc21   2001031117

This North American edition first published in 2001 by
Gareth Stevens Publishing
A World Almanac Education Group Company
330 West Olive Street, Suite 100
Milwaukee, WI 53212 USA

This U.S. edition © 2001 by Gareth Stevens, Inc. Original edition © 1999 by Franklin Watts.
First published as *How Many Are There?* in the series *Let's Explore* in 1999 by Franklin Watts,
96 Leonard Street, London, EC2A 4XD, United Kingdom. Additional end matter © 2001
by Gareth Stevens, Inc.

Series editor: Louise John
Series designer: Jason Anscomb
Series consultant: Peter Patilla
Gareth Stevens editor: Monica Rausch
Gareth Stevens designer: Katherine A. Kroll

Picture credits: Steve Shott Photography cover and title page, pp. 6, 11, 12, 13, 14, 15, 16,
19, 20, 22, 23, 24, 25, 27; Bubbles p. 26 (Jennie Woodcock); © M. Siluk/The Image Works
p. 29; Bruce Coleman pp. 8/9 (Jorg & Petra Wegner); Robert Harding p. 31; and Image Bank
p. 4 (Grant Faint).

With thanks to our models: Reid Burns, Karim Chehab, Alex Dymock, Melissa Eedle, Danielle
Grimmett-Gardiner, Charlie Newton, Robert Orbeney, and Alice Snedden.

Printed in the United States of America

1 2 3 4 5 6 7 8 9 05 04 03 02 01

Contents

One, two, three, four, five . . .
We can see numbers everywhere
we look — on the door of a house,
on the front of a bus, or on a
telephone. Where else can
you see numbers?

We can write numbers as figures or as words. For example, we can write the figure "1" or the word "one."

Can you match the words below with the figures opposite?

five two three four
six seven
eight nine ten

We can use numbers to count animals, such as these sheep.

How many sheep can you count?

When you first learned how to count, you probably used your fingers to help you count to ten. Maybe you used your toes, too!

11

How many oranges are on the plate?

Susan is adding two more oranges.
How many oranges
will be on the plate?

How many children are at this party?

Two children are ready to go home.

Take away, or subtract, two children. How many are left?

How many pieces of cake are on the plate? Divide the pieces of cake among the children so each child receives the same amount of cake. How many pieces of cake will each child have?

How many trucks do you see? If each truck has four wheels, what is the total number of wheels? If you said eight, you just multiplied two by four!

Sometimes we count objects in groups. A group of two objects is called a pair. What objects do we find in pairs?

How many shoes do you see?

Match the shoes to make pairs.

How many pairs can you make?

An even number, such as six, can be divided perfectly into pairs.

How many socks are
hanging on this clothesline?

How many pairs can you make?

An odd number, such as seven, cannot be divided perfectly into pairs. One object is always left over.

These boys are running a race. Joel finished first and won the race. Scott finished second, and Alan finished third.

Who will stand on block number one? Where will Alan stand? Where will Scott stand?

We can use numbers to measure weight, size, or distance. How many miles (kilometers) away is Barstow?

When we count lots and lots of things, such as people in a crowd, we use large numbers. What kinds of things would you count with the large numbers below?

100 – one hundred
1,000 – one thousand
1,000,000 – one million

Index

More Books to Read

Counting on Frank. Rod Clement (Gareth Stevens)
Each Orange Had Eight Slices. A Counting Book.
    Paul Giganti, Jr. (Greenwillow)
Math Curse. Jon Scieszka (Viking Children's Books)
Number Puzzles. First Step Math (series). Rose Griffiths
    (Gareth Stevens)